MAKE ME A
PRINCESS

Ticktock

MAKE ME A
PRINCESS

Contents

Contents

What makes a princess?

There's more to being a princess than wearing a sparkly tiara and a pretty dress. Being kind to others and having perfect manners are just as important as looking super-stylish!

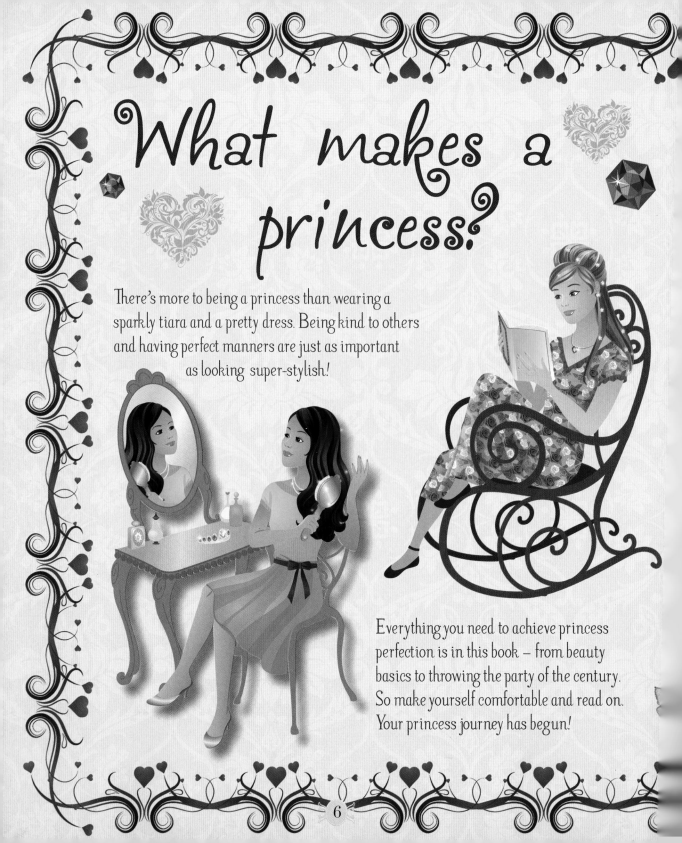

Everything you need to achieve princess perfection is in this book – from beauty basics to throwing the party of the century. So make yourself comfortable and read on. Your princess journey has begun!

a princess sparkles, whatever the occasion!

Your top-to-toe
transformation
starts here...

Your princess profile

Quiet and thoughtful or party-girl, what type of princess are you?

1. Who is your favourite fairytale princess?

a. Sleeping Beauty
b. Snow White
c. Cinderella

2. What would you wear to a royal ball?

a. A white silk gown and glass slippers
b. A floral frock and golden sandals
c. A red velvet dress and ruby shoes

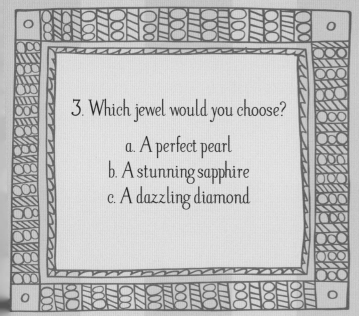

3. Which jewel would you choose?

    a. A perfect pearl
    b. A stunning sapphire
    c. A dazzling diamond

4. What would you call
a beautiful white pony?

    a. Magic Moonlight
    b. White Lightning
    c. Snow Dancer

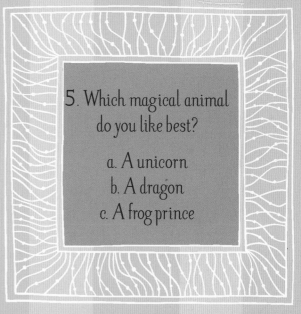

5. Which magical animal
do you like best?

    a. A unicorn
    b. A dragon
    c. A frog prince

Your profile

Count your a, b and c answers. Mostly a: Thoughtful and dreamy, you understand others and are a true friend. Mostly b: Loyal and brave, you love nature and care about our world. Mostly c: You're a party princess, who loves to meet and mingle. A mixture of a, b and c: Sensitive, lively and fun – you really are a perfect princess!

Get the look: princess fashion

For a true princess, fabulous fabrics and shimmering jewels are always in fashion, but each season also brings its own ideas and inspiration to keep her looking lovely all year long.

Read on for tips to set your own seasonal style.

Spring

Key colours for your spring wardrobe include daffodil yellow and pastel brights inspired by spring flowers. Think bluebell, primrose and cherry-blossom pink.

Buttoned-up, fitted winter styles are replaced by fluid fabric and a few frills and flounces.

Choose jewellery to complement your spring look. A gold tiara with glittering amethyst is perfect for petal pinks and soft purples. Or, choose a sparkling silver tiara with multi-coloured gems in this season's pretty pastels. Whatever the outfit, spring-time sparkle is a must!

Why not have fun with fashion motifs to suit your personality? Choose flowers, butterflies, stars, hearts or your own special theme to personalise your style.

Summer

For a princess who wants to look hot as well as cool, summer is a time for floaty fabrics in cute, candy colours.

Pinks and purples are girly but glam. Shimmering fabrics dazzle in bright sunlight, while jewellery can be bold, with large statement pieces.

note this fan-tastic way to keep cool!

To stay cool when it's hot, wear your hair off your face. Keep it tied back with sequin bands or flowing scarves for film-star chic.

sheer fabric is perfect for a light, fresh feel

Gold, jewelled sandals keep feet cool with strappy, snappy style. Glamorous sunglasses complete a sizzling summer look.

Autumn

When woodlands dazzle in shades of orange, yellow, red and brown, so does a season-savvy princess. These colours work together in any combination, while gold jewellery and accessories add to the mellow richness of autumnal shades.

leaf-shaped motifs work brilliantly

Layers are the answer to the season's changeable weather. A light wrap or shawl, thrown over your dress, gives warmth and swirly style.

Glittering golds combined with all shades of orange will give any girl an autumnal glow. Alternatively, try rich jewel colours instead. Sapphire blue or emerald green are perfect!

gold jewellery adds glamour to any autumn outfit

If you're a redhead, this is your season, but for everyone, shiny, tumbling locks are the way to go.

Winter

A princess is cool but she's never cold, because she dresses for the season and looks incredible – even in the most wintery weather.

Icy pinks and blues, shimmering silver and snowy white fill her wardrobe. Warm fabrics are super-important – wool and velvet give a luxurious look but are comfortable and cosy.

A swirling cloak trimmed with fun fake fur works over any princess dress, and a hood protects her shiny hair and twinkling tiara.

silver, platinum and diamonds add *icy sparkle*

ankle boots with fake fur trim are cute and cosy

pom-poms are pretty on princess pumps

Shoes

Just because your gown sweeps the floor, it doesn't mean you can forget about your feet! A flash of jewelled footwear looks divine, while sweet little satin ballet pumps suit almost any outfit.

dancing shoes help
princess toes to twinkle!

summer sandals studded
with jewels are perfect!

A princess knows that no girl can have
too many shoes. That's why she always has
the perfect pair for every royal occasion.

Bags

Every princess needs a few elegant essentials when she's out and about – and a beautiful bag to carry them. Choose one to match your dress or use it to add a pop of contrasting colour to your look.

a sweet *dolly bag* with feather trim

Don't forget your bag can be as decorative as your dress. Think jewels, sequins and silk flowers for evening and tassels, fringes and charms for daytime.

a classic *clutch* patterned with crystals

a *shoulder bag* for hands-free ease

Now design your own bag. Start by thinking about all the things you need to carry. Tissues? Lip gloss? A comb? Money? A spare tiara? A phone?

Then find some paper and draw your dream bag. Have fun with shape, colour and delicious detail.

Beauty secrets: princess pampering

Every princess knows that pampering is essential to keep her in tip-top shape. Looking after herself by eating healthily, getting plenty of fresh air and exercise, as well as making sure she gets her beauty sleep, means she always looks great!

Follow these beauty tips to make sure you glow from top-to-toe!

Magic facial massage

This relaxing step-by-step routine will make sure your face always has real princess radiance.

1 Sitting comfortably, use your middle fingers to make gentle circles on your temples.

2 Place your fingertips on your forehead, lightly and smoothly stroke to the sides.

3 With middle fingers, stroke along your eyebrows from above your nose to the ends.

4 Starting at your chin, very gently pinch along your jawline towards your ears.

5 With middle fingers, smooth down the sides of your nose in long strokes.

6 With your palms at jaw level, gently smooth upwards over your cheeks.

Sparkling eyes

Revive tired eyes and skin with this simple cucumber treatment.
You'll soon have your sparkle back!

You will need:

* small, clean jar with lid
* chopped cucumber*
* 2 cucumber slices
* cotton-wool pads
* water
* towel

An asterisk*, means always ask an adult to help you with this step.

1 Put the chopped cucumber and water in a jar. Pop it in the fridge to cool.

2 Dip a cotton-wool pad in the cucumber water and gently wipe it over your face.

3 Using a fresh pad, wipe carefully across your closed eyelids with the cool liquid.

4 Gently pat your face dry with a towel.

5 Lie down and relax with a cucumber slice on each of your closed eyes.

Wear sunglasses and protect your skin with sun cream in summer.

Nails...naturally

Make sure your fingers are always princess pretty with this simple routine.

You will need:
- nail file
- bowl of warm water
- towel
- hand cream

1 Gently file your nails into a pretty shape, smoothing off any rough edges.

2 Always file in one direction, not with a sawing motion, from the centre to the sides.

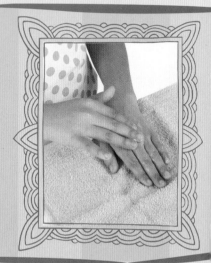

3 Soak your fingers in warm water for five minutes.

4 Dry your hands carefully and smooth hand cream generously over both hands.

5 Gently massage the back of each hand with the fingers of the other hand.

Princess polish

Here's how to apply polish perfectly for royal waving and greeting!

You will need:
* nail polish
* two hand towels
* nail polish remover
* cotton buds

1 Make sure your nails are clean and dry. Place one hand flat on an old towel.

2 Paint a stripe down the centre of each nail, with another stripe either side if necessary.

3 Wave your hands to your favourite pop song. Your nails will be dry by the end!

4 Use a little remover on a cotton bud to clean up if you make tiny mistakes.

Dazzling designs

Here are some fun ideas for party-perfect nails. Try them, then invent some of your own!

You will need:

* nail polishes
* nail gems and stickers

1 Paint your nails and, once they are dry, add nail stickers for instant glamour.

2 Or, while the polish is still tacky, gently add flowers or other nail art.

3 Once you have finished, add a final coat of clear polish to keep your funky designs looking brilliant!

Perfect princess pedicure

You will need:
- large bowl of warm water
- body or foot lotion
- towel
- nail clippers
- nail file
- nail polish (optional)

Here's how to make sure your feet look fabulous all summer long.

1 Soak your feet for five minutes in the warm water.

2 Dry your feet carefully, especially between your toes!

3 Trim toenails straight across with clippers and smooth with a file if necessary.

4 Massage lotion into your feet, avoiding your nails if you want to paint them.

Apply polish in a pretty colour.
Don't try to put on your shoes until it's really dry!

Crowning glory: taming your lovely locks

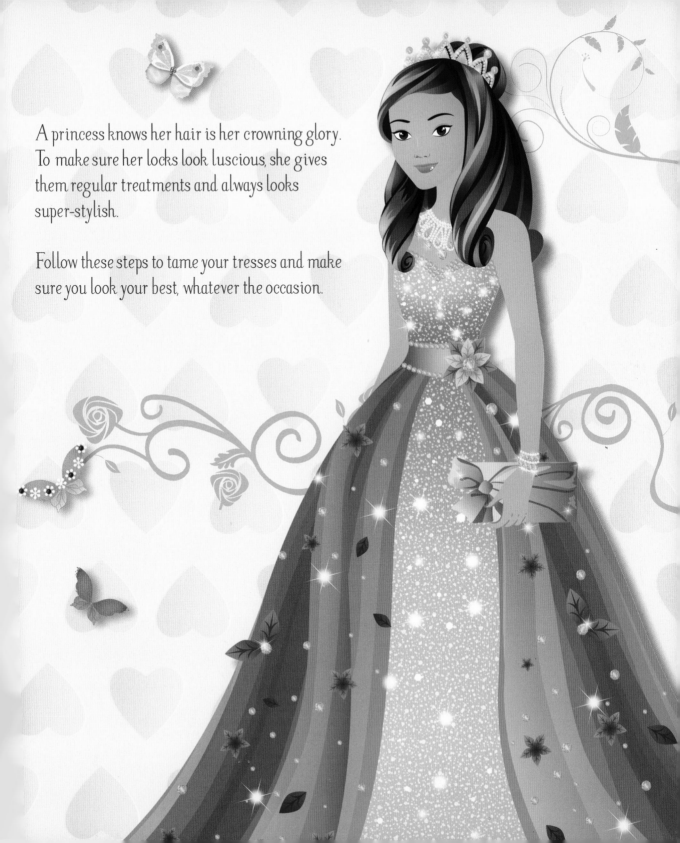

A princess knows her hair is her crowning glory. To make sure her locks look luscious, she gives them regular treatments and always looks super-stylish.

Follow these steps to tame your tresses and make sure you look your best, whatever the occasion.

Treat your tresses

These fragrant herbal treatments will give your lovely locks natural princess beauty.

For fair hair you will need:

- bowl
- towel
- 1 camomile tea bag
- mug of hot water

1 Put the tea bag and water in the bowl. Leave to cool while you wash your hair as usual.

2 Pour the water over your hair. Rinse, then wrap your hair in a towel to dry.

For red or dark hair you will need:

- bowl
- 2–3 sprigs of rosemary
- mug of hot water
- towel

1 Put the rosemary and water in the bowl. Wash your hair as usual while it cools.

2 Pour the water over your hair. Rinse, then wrap your hair in a towel to dry.

Princess spring style

This sweet and simple fishtail plait can be decorated for extra impact.

You will need:

- brush or comb
- styling spray
- a hair band
- accessories to decorate

1 Gently brush your hair until it is smooth and tangle-free.

2 Spritz your hair all over with the styling spray.

3 Divide the top into two sections. Wrap a small piece from under the right section over and to the left.

4 Repeat with a piece from under the left side. Keep alternating sides, securing the end with a band.

It's easier if you plait
a princess pal's hair
and she does yours!

Simple summer style

There is nothing like blow-drying for achieving a natural, swingy style, just right for summer.

You will need:

- ❀ towel
- ❀ styling spray
- ❀ hair clips
- ❀ round brush
- ❀ hairdryer
- ❀ hairspray

1 Shampoo and condition your hair as usual, then gently towel dry.

2 Spritz your slightly damp hair lightly all over with styling spray.

3 Starting at the back, take one section of hair and clip the rest out of the way.

4 Direct the hairdryer on to the section and slowly brush through it until dry.

5 As you finish a section, spritz it with hairspray, until your summer style is complete!

Autumn waves

Here's the perfect look for windswept autumn – tumbling tantalising waves to toss.

You will need:

* hair clips
* styling spray
* round brush
* hairdryer
* hairspray

1 Brush clean, dry hair, then pin the hair on top of your head out of the way.

2 Generously spritz the ends on the lower layer with styling spray.

3 Take a small section, wrap the spritzed hair round the brush and dry it thoroughly.

4 Move on, a section at a time, until all the hair, including the top layer, has been waved.

5 Use plenty of hairspray to kee your curls until you are ready to wash or brush them out.

Winter glamour

This stunning style is super-fast but perfect for sparkling evening parties.

You will need:
- brush or comb
- 4 hair bands
- hair grips and clips

1 Pull your hair into a low ponytail. Secure it with a hair band.

2 Divide the ponytail into three strands. Divide the strands into three again and make three plaits.

3 Curl one of the plaits round and pin it into place using hair grips.

4 Twist the other plaits in the same way and secure into a bun with hair grips.

Add sparkling clips or hair jewels for evening glamour.

The ultimate up-do

Here's a sophisticated style that makes you the belle of any ball with real princess pizzazz.

You will need:

- brush or comb
- hair band
- hair grips and clips
- hair donut
- hairspray

1 Brush your hair up to make a ponytail on the very top of your head.

2 Pull your ponytail gently through the centre of the donut.

3 Wrap your hair over and around the donut.

4 Tuck in the ends and secure everything with hair grips so that the bun is firm.

5 Add flowers to decorate and use hairspray to smooth down any short, flyaway hairs.

Perfect princess twists

With a princess pal to help you, this sweet style is simplicity itself.

You will need:

* brush or comb
* 2 hair bands
* hair grips
* flower clip
* a friend to help!!

1 Ask your friend to take a front section of your hair and divide it into two.

2 Twist the right half over and over the left all the way to the bottom.

3 Pin up the first twist and make a second twist on the same side, as shown.

4 Repeat steps 2 and 3 on the other side.

5 Once you have finished the twists, hold them in place using hair bands.

This style's pretty decorated with a lovely flower clip!

Sixty-second styles

Every princess needs some quick fixes when she wants to be ready in a magic minute.

To change her style in seconds, a true princess always has in her bag:

- hairbrush or comb
- headscarf
- hair band
- flower clip
- spare tiara!

1 Brush your hair over to one side and make a low ponytail. Simple and sweet.

2 Use a pretty scarf as a headband for an instant Hollywood hairdo.

3 Add instant drama with a larger-than-life flower clip.

4 A single high ponytail is slick and sophisticated.

5 Pull your hair into a low ponytail, plait it and add flowers for a fresh look.

If in doubt, a tiara adds a touch of class to any hairstyle!

Sparkling jewels and twinkling tiaras

Princesses always sparkle, but they can't resist adding gorgeous gems and jewels to their outfit for truly glittering glamour.

Choosing the right jewellery is as vital as selecting a stunning gown. Read on to find out how to pick the right accessories to make sure you shimmer and shine, whatever the occasion!

Which jewel is right for you?

January: a deep red garnet

February: a delicate purple amethyst

Enjoy choosing gems to match your eyes, your dress or your mood – or choose your princess birthstone for a special signature sparkle.

March: a shimmering green-blue aquamarine

April: a glittering diamond

May: a gorgeous green emerald

June: a pure white pearl

July: a rich red ruby

August: a glowing green peridot

September: a brilliant blue sapphire

October: an amazing multi-coloured opal

November: an awesome orange topaz

December: an ocean-blue turquoise

Genuine jewels make you feel like a million dollars – and may cost as much! Fakes are just as fabulous, and much lighter on the bank balance!

Design your own tiara

A true princess doesn't set foot outside the palace without her tiara... made from the finest gold or silver and studded with a host of glittering jewels. What kind of tiara would you choose to crown your perfect princess look?

Use these tempting tiaras as inspiration, then draw your own perfect headpiece.

stick on sequins for extra sparkle!

stick-on gems will give your tiara a really royal finish!

Add glitter for that extra bit of bling

Dazzling rings

You will need:
- pipecleaner
- pencil
- glitter glue or stick-on jewels

Make fabulous flower rings for every finger with this easy princess project.

1 Starting 5cm from the end of the pipecleaner, wrap it round the pencil then twist it once to make a loop.

2 Keep making loops next to each other until you have six in a row.

3 Bend the loops round into a circle and twist the ends once to secure.

4 Twist the ends together into a ring shape to fit your finger. Add glitter glue or stick-on jewels to decorate.

Make a range of
rings to add glitz to
any gown.

Pretty button bracelet

1 Cut a piece of elastic long enough to wrap around your wrist twice.*

2 Choose buttons for your bracelet. Thread the elastic through two holes on each button so they lie flat.

3 Knot the ends of the elastic to fit your wrist. Add glitter glue or stick-on jewels for gorgeous glamour.

Choose *dazzling* colours to complement your clothes.

Princess pendants

Express your princess personality by designing your very own pendant in scintillating silver.

You will need:

- cardboard
- scissors*
- string
- aluminium foil
- PVA glue
- jewels or glitter glue
- ribbon or cord

An asterisk*, means always ask an adult to help you with this step.

1 Cut a shape from cardboard. Pierce a hole in the top edge. Brush glue over one side.*

2 Use string to make a pretty pattern like the one above – or design your own.

3 Leave to dry. Then brush on more glue and lay foil on top.

4 Press the foil down very gently with your fingers.

5 Use jewels or glitter glue to decorate your pendant, then thread it on to the ribbon.

Princess friendship bracelets

1 Take three coloured ribbons, cords or strands of wool about 40cm long.

2 Knot the strands 4cm from one end. Put a heavy book on the knot. Spread out the strands.

3 Put the strand on the left over the middle one. Then put the one on the right over the middle one.

4 Keep going (left, right, left, right) to the end. Knot the end, then give your bracelet to a friend!

Tie the bracelet to your princess pal's wrist and hope she's made one for you, too! An armful of bracelets shows you're a popular princess!

Make a princess petal brooch

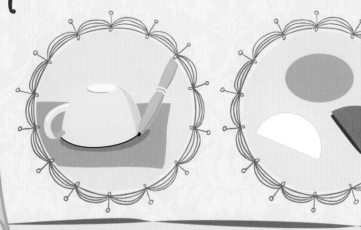

1 Using the cup, draw five circles on the fabric and cut them out.*

2 Fold each circle in half, then half again, with the right side outside.

3 Take one piece and stitch around the curved edge.*

4 Gently pull the thread to gather the fabric into a petal shape.*

5 Without cutting the thread, do the same with the other petals.*

6 Stitch the last petal to the first to make a flower shape.*

7 Use PVA glue to fix a jewel or pretty button to the flower centre.

add ribbon to make a pretty bracelet

Sew a safety-pin or hair clip to the back to flaunt your fab flower.*

Plush palaces:
homes fit
for a
princess

When a princess isn't partying or performing her royal duties, she needs a place to lay her pretty head. Her perfect palace looks luxurious but feels homely. It's as lovely as she is – and just as warm and inviting.

Read on to find out how to turn your bedroom into a room fit for a princess.

Your dream palace

Think about your princess life. Will you need a window in a turret for Rapunzel moments? Or a glittering ballroom for the party of the century?

Use the amazing mansions on the right to inspire you as you sketch out a design for your own perfect palace.

don't forget a *balcony* for royal appearances

design a royal standard

decorate your palace with sparkling jewels

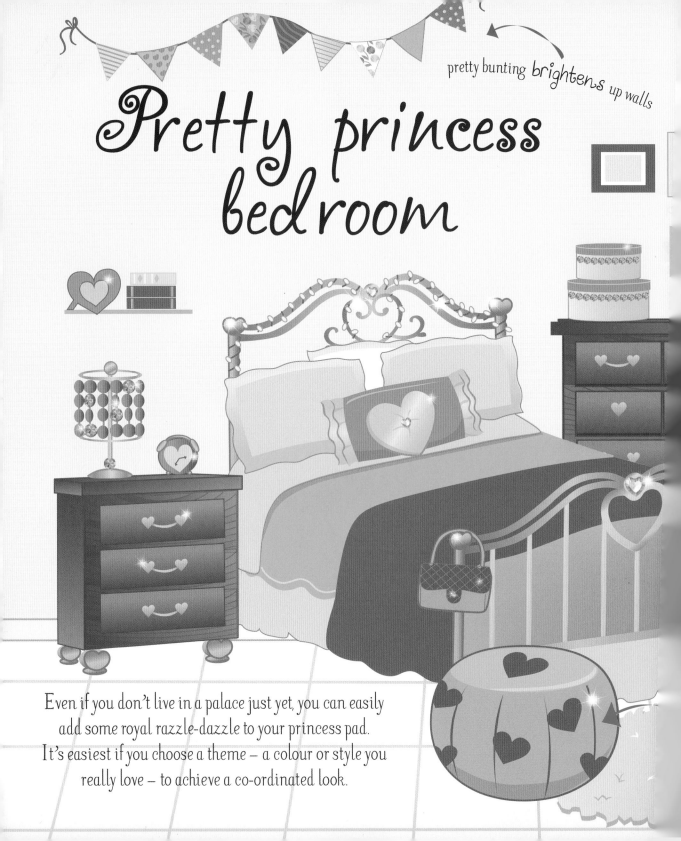

pretty bunting *brightens* up walls

Pretty princess bedroom

Even if you don't live in a palace just yet, you can easily add some royal razzle-dazzle to your princess pad. It's easiest if you choose a theme – a colour or style you really love – to achieve a co-ordinated look.

jazz up your walls with *fun* frames

matching accessories add instant *glamour*

Treasure box

A princess needs somewhere to keep her jewels, her letters from Prince Charming and her secret diary. Make your own special box.

1 Mix equal amounts of bright paint and PVA glue and brush it over an old shoe box. Leave it to dry.

2 Decorate it with stickers, ribbons, buttons, stick-on jewels, coloured foil or tissue-paper flowers.

3 Be creative with your design by adding a crown or star in the decoration, outlined in glitter.

4 Using PVA glue, attach wrapping paper to the inside of the box to make a pretty lining.

use it to keep your *diary* and precious things safe!

Perfect photo frame

A heart-shaped frame shows how much you LOVE being a princess!

You will need:

- a pencil
- 2 pieces of card, the same size
- scissors*
- glue or sticky tape
- coloured paper or stickers

An asterisk*, means always ask an adult to help you with this step.

1 Draw a heart shape on one piece of card and cut it out carefully.*

2 Use glue or sticky tape to stick the two pieces of card together on three sides. Leave the top open.

3 Decorate the frame with coloured paper or stickers. Slide a photo or drawing into the frame from the top.

make a hole in the top of the card and thread a pretty *ribbon* through the hole and tie it in a bow to hang it up!

Bedroom bunting

1 Mark the mid-point on each edge of the card with a pencil.

2 Use a ruler to join the marks. Then cut out this diamond shape.*

3 Trace round the template on the back of the wrapping paper.

4 Cut out the diamond shapes and fold each one in half.*

5 Slip the shapes over the string and glue the folds together.

Bunting
adds instant glamour.
It's perfect for parties!

On your best
behaviour: perfect
princess
poise

Are princesses too posh to be polite? No way! A princess is always friendly and poised, putting people she meets at ease. She treats others as she would like to be treated – and everyone loves her for it.

Here's how to have perfect princess poise, whatever the occasion...

Princess Ps and Qs

A princess always minds her Ps and Qs or 'pleases' and 'thank-yous', of course, but it's not just when she's speaking that Ps and Qs are part of her princess polish.

Banqueting behaviour

It doesn't matter if she's dining at a banquet or taking tea for two. A real princess knows how to mind her manners.

she never talks with her mouth full

she listens politely even if the chat is a bit dull!

she uses the correct cutlery, working from the outside in

A princess makes sure that everyone around her feels comfortable
– and that's really what good manners are all about.
She's never too grand to have a good time.

she chats to people on *both* sides

she has *fun* and enjoys the party!

Being kind to others

A princess never forgets that she is privileged to live in a palace with everything her heart desires. She knows that helping others gives her even more pleasure than pleasing herself.

She is the first to volunteer when a charity needs helpers. She'll rattle a collecting tin, bake princess cakes for sale, or help with publicity.

Whether it's ailing animals or poorly people, a true princess is always ready to help others. She's quick to offer her princess possessions to charities when she doesn't need them and she cares about the environment, too.

a charity ball puts the *fun* in fundraising!

ROYAL CHARITY BALL

Curtsey like a princess

1 Bow your head to show respect and hold the sides of your skirt.

2 Put your right foot a little behind your left foot, with your right heel off the ground.

3 Gracefully bend your knees and slowly lower yourself down.

4 Just as gracefully, rise again to stand up straight.

a prince bows by nodding his head and bringing his shoulders forward slightly,

as you curtsey slowly and elegantly...

practice in a mirror and you will be the curtsey queen in no time!

Parties, princess-style

A perfect princess simply has to be the hostess with the mostest. She's charming, welcoming and warm – and her parties are talked about for years afterwards.

Princess parties appear effortless, but a lot of work goes on behind the scenes. Luckily, as any savvy socialite knows, there are tips and tricks that will make any event amazing.

Invitations

Truly enticing invitations have two vital ingredients – info and allure. In other words, they tell your guests everything they need to know: the time, place, event, dress code, address for reply and so on and they must be... well... inviting!

a decorative edging is princess pretty

HRH Princess Paula
invites you to a
Grand Imperial Ball

7.30pm this Saturday
at the Pink Palace

RSVP: Pink Palace 12345

tell your guests what to bring

Please come to my
amaZZZZing sleepover!

This Saturday at 7pm.
Bring a sleeping bag
and a teddy bear!

RSVP:
hrh@princessmail.com

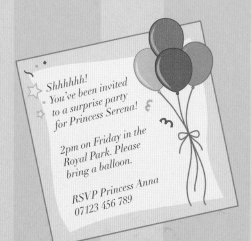

Shhhhhh!
You've been invited
to a surprise party
for Princess Serena!

2pm on Friday in the
Royal Park. Please
bring a balloon.

RSVP Princess Anna
07123 456 789

RSVP means please reply!

Buy pretty cards or make your own to match the theme of the party.

Have fun with your invitations. Use glitter to add sparkle, and play with shapes and colours. How about a royal scroll for a special party?

Pre-party pamper

When her party is perfectly planned and prepared, a princess has time before her guests arrive to de-stress and make sure she's looking her radiant best.

You will need:

* a warm bath*
* cup of oatmeal (fine is best)
* pair of old tights or a pop sock
* scissors*

An asterisk*, means always ask an adult to help you with this step.

1 Cut the foot from a clean pair of old tights, about 20cm long. Pour in the oatmeal and tie the top.*

2 Add the bag to a warm bath, squeezing it gently if you like.

3 Lie back and relax in a blissful bath for super-soft skin. Now you're ready... to get ready!

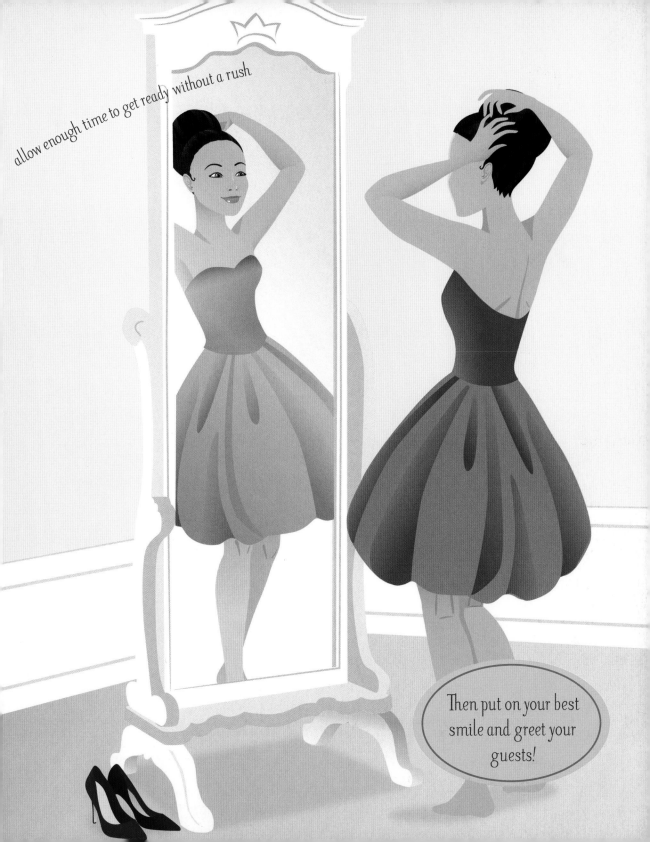

allow enough time to get ready without a rush

Then put on your best smile and greet your guests!

Princess party

Every party is different. Don't be afraid to borrow ideas from events you've enjoyed. Remember: if your guests are happy and you're having fun, it's a perfect princess party!

confetti looks great on tables!

Summer fruits look *stylish!*

welcome your guests with a drink

no party is complete without music!

It's fun to have a theme for the food and drink. Pink, perhaps?
Cranberry juice and lemonade makes the perfect princess punch
while pink and purple cupcakes will tempt your guests!

Party games

Get the party started with some great music and giggly games. They're perfect for breaking the ice and introducing people who don't know each other.

For 'The Name Game', put a simple paper headband on each guest. Each has to guess the name on their band by asking others questions but answers can only be 'yes' or 'no'.

For 'Sleeping Beauties', everyone lies down and pretends to sleep. 'The Prince' makes jokes and comments. The winner, who keeps still longest, is crowned 'Sleeping Beauty'.

You've played 'Pin the tail on the donkey' but how about 'Stick the glass slipper on Cinderella'?

Super sleepovers

When you want to get together with your princess pals, there's nothing better than a palace sleepover.

Choose a theme you'll all enjoy and don't forget that even princesses need their beauty sleep!

Choose a princess movie to watch – or even two!

make princess pink popcorn!

Give a prize for the most princessy pyjamas!

Supply a few simple craft materials and make your own crazy crowns!

use fruit, ice cream and sprinkles to create Cinderella sundaes

make cupcakes and decorate them

Sleepover style

Why not host a style sleepover? Set up your bedroom as a beauty parlour and invite your princess pals to give each other facials, manicures, massages, hair-styles and make-up sessions. Look back at pages 24 to 55 for ideas.

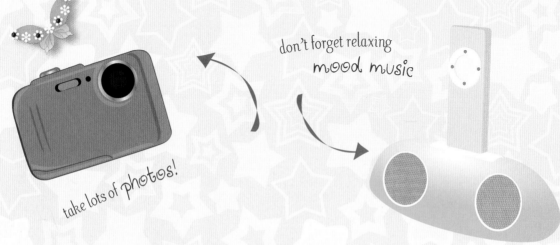

don't forget relaxing *mood music*

take lots of *photos!*

pink towels and toiletries are perfect!

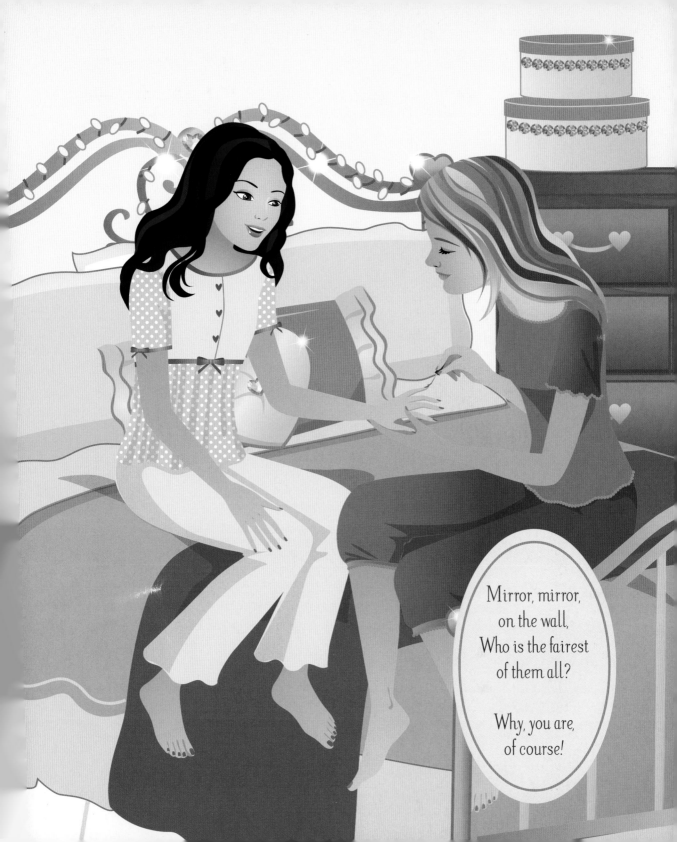

Mirror, mirror,
on the wall,
Who is the fairest
of them all?

Why, you are,
of course!

Travelling in style

When a princess leaves her palace for a party, she needs to travel in style, in something that suits her royal position and has room for a billowing ballgown.

In spring a glass coach is light and airy but keeps seasonal showers at bay.

An open carriage is dreamy for travelling to a midsummer night's ball.

Autumn requires a golden coach to suit the season's hues.

In winter, a sumptuous sleigh is the cosy way to travel through thick snow.

Design your perfect carriage

Design the carriage of your dreams, whether it is made of gold, glass or ebony, large enough for your friends or just one perfect prince and drawn by six gleaming black horses or a single white stallion, you can let your imagination go wild!

Don't forget to design the inside of your carriage,
too. Will you sit on cream leather seats or relax on
red velvet? Perhaps your carriage will have cushions
to curl up with, decorated with bows, tassels,
or buttons.

What type of handles will your carriage have?
Clear crystal or glorious gold? Your feet will need
a plush princess fabric to rest on, in a traditional
coronet pattern, or something modern and stylish.
The design decisions are yours!

The perfect prince

Perhaps you've met him
already, or simply seen him in
your dreams. Whatever your
perfect prince is like, one thing
is certain: for him, you'll be the
only princess in the world.

Prince predictor

Here's a fun way to find out what your perfect prince will
be like and how you will meet him.

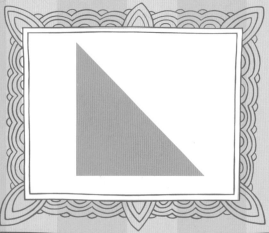

1 Fold a square of paper in half to make a triangle, then again to make a smaller triangle.

2 Open out the paper and fold each corner into the middle, making a square. Turn over and repeat.

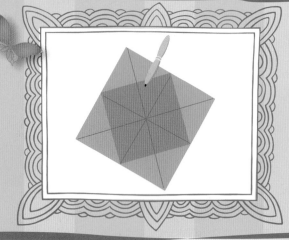

3 Unfold it and write your answers on the flaps, using the suggestions opposite or make up your own!

4 Put your first finger and thumb of each hand in the flaps of the predictor to open and close it.

What to write on your predictor:

Front flaps – hair colour: blonde; brown; red; black

Inside flaps – personality: sporty; friendly; generous; thoughtful; romantic; caring; kind; brave

Under inside flaps – where you'll meet: at a ball; at a banquet; out riding; on a yacht; at a wedding; at a garden party; at a concert; at a royal picnic

Your dream princess wedding

Every girl is a princess on her wedding day, but the marriage of a real princess is truly amazing. Every part of it has to be just perfect.

don't forget to design a cake and bouquet!

However the bride wears her hair, it's *tiara time!*

her dress glitters with sequins or crystals

On her wedding day, a princess bride is radiant. Imagine what your wedding will be like!

Now draw your own wedding dress. Will it be a full, fairy tale classic style or a sleek, modern design?

How to dance like Cinderella

1 Put your left hand on your prince's shoulder and your right in his hand at shoulder height.

2 Step back on your right foot, then back and to the left with your left, followed by your right foot.

3 Step forward with the left foot, then forward and right with your right, followed by your left foot.

4 Just keep repeating steps 2 and 3, following your prince's lead, as you slowly move around the dance floor.

your prince will steer you around the floor

Rate your princess progress

It's time to take the final test to see if you have what it takes to be a true princess!

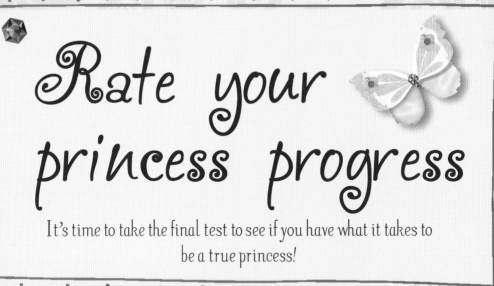

1. You long to see your princess pals. What do you invite them to?
a. A sleepover?
b. A picnic?
c. A grand ball?

2. It's your wedding day! What is most important to you?
a. That all the people who have queued to see you have a good view?
b. That the sun shines all day long?
c. That your dress and hair look perfect?

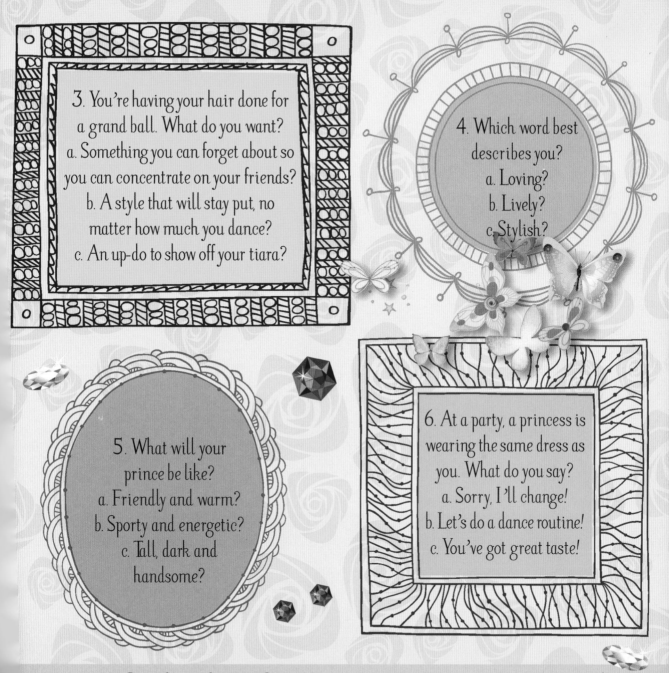

3. You're having your hair done for a grand ball. What do you want?
a. Something you can forget about so you can concentrate on your friends?
b. A style that will stay put, no matter how much you dance?
c. An up-do to show off your tiara?

4. Which word best describes you?
a. Loving?
b. Lively?
c. Stylish?

5. What will your prince be like?
a. Friendly and warm?
b. Sporty and energetic?
c. Tall, dark and handsome?

6. At a party, a princess is wearing the same dress as you. What do you say?
a. Sorry, I'll change!
b. Let's do a dance routine!
c. You've got great taste!

Answers

Count your a, b and c answers. Mostly a: Well done! You're a people person, a friend to everyone – a real princess. Mostly b: Congratulations! You have the energy and fun factor of a true princess. Mostly c: Excellent! Beautiful and poised, you're everyone's idea of a real princess. A mixture of a, b and c: Sensational! You've got it all, your royal highness!

Your top-to-toe princess checklist

Before you step out of your palace, make a quick check that you are princess perfect.

your hair is *shiny* and *styled*

you are poised and *smiling!*

your skin is *clear* and *glowing*

your jewellery *sparkles!*

your feet and hands are *lovely!*

your dress has princess *pizzazz!*

Now you know all there is to being a princess it's time to live...

happily ever after!

Princess words

Balcony
A small platform outside a building, reached from a window

Carriage
A four-wheeled vehicle pulled by two or more horses.

Charm (1)
A small metal decoration or jewel

Charm (2)
Attractiveness

Chic
Stylish and elegant

Chiffon
Very light, sheer fabric

Clutch bag
A small bag with no strap

Coach
A state carriage, used for important occasions

Confetti
Tiny pieces of coloured paper or petals to throw at celebrations

Conveyance
A vehicle

Dolly bag
A bag with a drawstring to close it

Ebony
A kind of wood, nearly black in colour

Fabric
Woven, knitted or felted material

Fairytale
A magical story with a happy ending

Fan
Paper stretched over a frame that you wave to make a cooling breeze

Floral
Covered or filled with flowers

Fringe
A border of hanging threads

Gem
A precious stone, cut to make it shine

Glamour
Magical beauty

Jewel
An ornament with precious stones

Luxurious
Expensive and enjoyable

Mansion
A grand house

Motif
A small design idea

Palace
A grand home for important people, such as princesses

Pastel
A light colour

Poise
Calm, controlled, thoughtful behaviour

Pompom
A round ornament made of tightly bunched ribbons, threads or flowers

Princess
A royal girl or woman, often the daughter of a king, queen, prince or princess

Privileged
Having special advantages

Pump
A light, flat shoe for dancing or sports

Radiant
Dazzling or glowing

Season
Time of year: winter, spring, summer or autumn

Sequin
A tiny, shiny decoration

Shawl
A large piece of material, usually worn draped over the shoulders or head

Sheer
Almost see-through or transparent

Shoulder bag
A bag with a long strap

Sleigh
A vehicle with runners instead of wheels for travelling over snow, pulled by horses, dogs or reindeer

Standard
A flag

Tassel
An ornament made of a bunch of hanging threads

Tiara
A small, light crown or band, usually very sparkly

Train
A long piece of material stretching from the back of a dress, which may drag along the ground or be carried by servants

Turret
A small tower in a castle or palace

Volunteer
Someone who offers to work without payment

Index

An Hachette UK Company
www.hachette.co.uk

First published in Great Britain in 2013 by Ticktock,
an imprint of Octopus Publishing Group Ltd
Endeavour House
189 Shaftesbury Avenue
London
WC2H 8JY
www.octopusbooks.co.uk
www.ticktockbooks.co.uk

ISBN 978 1 84898 937 5

A CIP record for this book is available from the British Library

Printed and bound in China
1 3 5 7 9 10 8 6 4 2

Author: Nicola Baxter Artists: Anita Romeo and Diane Kolar
Series Editor: Sue McMillan Design: Alison Gadsby
Publisher: Tim Cook Managing Editor: Karen Rigden Production: Lucy Carter

Photography: Gavin Sawyer for Roddy Paine Studios

But Elephant wasn't excited. He didn't think
his brother was cuddly, cute or handsome.
He thought he was **horrid**!

Mum said that when Elephant's brother got bigger, they would **have fun** together. Grandma said they could **share toys**. Dad said they could **play games** together.